# The Will and the Grace

for Norma —
I send you my
love and my prayer
for all good to fill
your life.
Warmly,
Diane

OTHER BOOKS BY DIANE WESTLAKE

Gentle Freedom

Gentle Freedom, Gentle Courage

# THE WILL AND THE GRACE

ILLISTRATIONS BY JULIE GALAS

By Diane Westlake

DEDICATION: To those who love for no return. . . who heal society as they send forth love from one androgynous soul.

Library of Congress Catalogue Number: 169-882
ISBN: 0-9614438-0-4

Acknowledgments: Thanks to Evelyn DeSpain, Bobi Ferguson, Douglas Pagels, Lydia Walker, Bob Westby, Patty Woods, Laurel Woodson. Special thanks to Julie Galas for all art work.

For poet jonivan. . . in remembrance . . . we lovingly say "Thank You".

Printed in the United States of America: Blake Printery, San Luis Obispo, California

Fen Winnie Ink
P.O. Box 13658
San Luis Obispo, CA 93406

# CONTENTS

## FROM THE AUTHOR

It is my intent that each reader of this book will find a word, a phrase, a poem, or the complete book which each of you will keep with you for your entire life. I put my trust in my desire to offer, to you, a new thought, a new concept and a new way of seeing yourself, of seeing others, and of living in our society with peace in your heart.

There is love for each one of you in every word I have written. Please receive, from this book, any and all feelings and thoughts that can assist you into a comfortable way of being. Let us share our love and positive thoughts with each other during this life journey, and let us bring joy, comfort, peace and harmony to ALL others as we travel this plane together.

*Diane Westlake*

# PRELUDE

The beginning of all good is love. The middle and the end, the ultimate offering is love. That which each person seeks, with which each one grows and heals is love. Love is what every individual wishes to give, to offer as a life contribution. . . the sharing of a loving heart.

In the troubled cycles of every century, every generation, every change of the governing bodies or individuals in our Universe, negative energy, doubt, suffering and fear are stirred to rise to the surface spreading negative thinking to blanket the majority of the populations of this planet.

The media reports horror and atrocity. Writers and poets pen out the reflections of anger, outrage and mistrust of their fellows. Amid all of this can be heard an occasional voice teaching positive thought and the opposites of fear. Lately, more voices have joined the chorus in teaching positive creation of a joyous prosperous life. . . a life filled with comfort and hope.

No matter what the source of these voices. . . whether the churches or the commercial consciousness groups which are forming throughout our continents. . . these spiritual words are the repetition or paraphrasing of the ancient Laws. . . "The Way". . . of the centuries old philosophies of Tao, Hinduism, Buddhism and other Eastern disciplines. All modern day spiritual groups are echoes of the Universal Laws of consciousness and spirituality.

Everything presented in the written and spoken word has its place to be seen or heard. Without the negative the people would not be so eagerly and magnetically attracted to the positive. This book *The Will and the Grace* is fashioned to present in concise and poetic form many of the tried and applied Universal Laws. Poetry is shorter than hundreds of pages of metaphysical or "self-help" consciousness books. Poetry affords the reader the opportunity to fit the Laws and concepts to the flow of each individual's life. Poetry's beauty and opportunity for the use of poetic license gives readers the freedom to stretch and mold every word, every line, to their particular life situations.

In interweaving love, compassion, acceptance, non-judgement, non-resistance and trust throughout these writings, I have put into action one of the most fundamental Universal Laws. That is, in order to keep love (or any positive quality) we must give it away . . . to everyone. We must give it away to keep it. Hearing the Laws, implanting them in our brains and repeating them are only small measures of the process of using them. To live the Laws, to "walk what we talk," to work with these Laws (in order to create our own lives), to grow into higher consciousness as a result of absorbing the concepts into our total being takes all of this lifetime in addition to all other lives spent incarnate in human form.

There are times when some Laws are not even recognized because we are not ready for them. There are times when we may memorize a Law using it as an affirmation, yet it is impossible to live it because it is not yet time in the sequence of our own personal development. We build a foundation, Law upon Law, according to our individual growth. Each one of us will acquire the use of the Laws in order of the pattern of our degree or level of consciousness and spirituality. We cannot "know" what we do not yet "know" no matter how many times it is repeated in the written or spoken word.

This does not mean limitation in ourselves. It means patience. . . to recognize and function within the Divine Order, the Divine Timing of the Divine Plan. And no amount of pushing against time or holding our mouths right will hasten assimilation of the Laws into our lives.

Seeing and hearing the Laws in repetition, in affirmation, will aid the constancy of exposure so that these truths are an ever present conditioning rhythm in our minds. The positive thought and use of these words of truth will begin to reshape our lives. Because of the fact that repetition of positive thought negates any possibility of time for negative thoughts, all resentments, hurts, angers, frustrations, jealousies, despair and sorrow lessen and fade for lack of use in thought time.

The positive thoughts of the Universal Laws of Consciousness are the Perennial Philosophy and this age old philosophy fills our hours and days creating calm, trust, compassion, integrity, love, unconditional love and the goal of enlightenment.

Many books have been written recently in the name of "new thought." Rather than write yet another "self help" text, I have chosen to bring the Universal Laws, the Perennial Philosophy, to you in the form of free verse poetry. Most poetry as we have known it throughout history recants the sorrow, misery, anger and fear of the negative side of the lives of poets. Although each one of us finds a piece of our own life in those works, with which we can (and do) identify, we stay steeped in negative thought and feeling as we read and reread words of pain, fear and anger.

For health, growth, success and a life with greater peace in our inner person, this book brings the truths of the Laws to lift us, to raise our Spirits and our goals, to free us from fear and bring us peace in this life's journey through will and grace.

# THE WILL

The search for truth begins. Our will and willpower now come into action. We must be willing to bring to our lives the discipline of taking responsibility for our own actions. We must be willing to release old habits and desires. The understanding that every person is responsible for his or her life, as we are responsible for our own life, becomes a constant force in our consciousness as the quest begins.

Courage, open-mindedness, strength and perseverance are now tools for progress on this path of our quest. And "will", the power which has always been ours, is activated for our good and the good of others. We always have a choice. We have already chosen our life and we have the choice, the free will, to keep or change any part of it. With this knowing, our "will" must call into action the flexibility necessary for coming changes. Once one foot is on the path, the journey has begun and changes will occur in our lives with precise certainty. We have asked for truth, evolvement, higher consciousness and spirituality. Only we can attain these gifts for ourselves. We guide our own lives through change, sometimes by taking the "holy risks", sometimes by releasing people from our lives whose paths are not parallel with ours.

Along our path we must release negative energy in the form of old ideas or habits. At times we release a person or group of people who generate negative energy. This is the time to "love away" negativity. For it is a truth that when we surround negative energy with love, it either changes or goes away. Negative energy can be people, situations or concepts. To move past negativity we put out an abundance of love. Fear, judgment and resentment change nothing. Love changes everything. If the negative force is to be a part of our quest, it will change to positive loving energy. If it is not to be a part of our life, at this time, it will go away. "Will" has been exercised, choice has been made, change has taken place. For negativity cannot abide in the higher vibration of loving energy.

There is within each of us our Christ Self. This higher self must now give permission to our worldly self to move onward and upward through learning, knowing and living the Universal Laws of Consciousness. . . of the Perennial Philosophy.

During this process will come the period of cleansing mentally, physically, emotionally and spiritually. The cleansing of the temple of our spirit makes room for all that is new. . . new growth, new concepts, new habits, new people, a new way of life and a new place to be.

Willing all of this. . . making the commitment to ourselves and our Higher Power. . . we have begun the quest. Truth and love surround us and are there in unlimited supply. We need only open ourselves to receive them. And we will.

**L**ook to the future
though you suffer now
it will not be this way
always

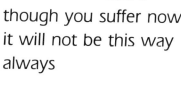

**N**o matter how white your truth
how high your guidance
It is
the way you walk through life
and how you treat others
which are the measures
of your growth

**W**hen all of this has past
you will know time has taken course
change comes to end this part of life
beginnings now are yours by choice
your plan revolves. . . unfolds. . . renews
step by step reaching higher levels
part pain. . . some knowing
asking. . . surrender. . . love and trust
each cycle giving promise that time has come
Move on brave spirit face all challenge
move up soul courageous learn anew
Speak the Laws and follow
Live the Laws and lead
Always safe always free going forward
swift and brightest light you are evolving
in the quiet of this moment
with the newness of your self
look around and find
that all the rest has past

The soft strong women
women of our age and ages past
moving through humanities of the hour
quiet strength and silent courage
mothers of the people. . . mothers together
soft. . . the tenderness and gentle
Yet should need for power arise
the soft strong women
come from the depth of the cylinder
the core of the primitive being
animal and goddess
bringing forth all magnificence
mightiest force of the Universe
girding, supporting, moving, challenging, changing
the first. . . the last. . . unleashed storms of strength
relentless until the work is done
Then quietly. . . peacefully returning serenity
soft. . . the tenderness and gentle
mother to mother to man to all
circles so wholly the nurturing
resting
the soft strong women

Non-resistance
battles unfought yet situations saved
standing silent in the face of unfairness
passive powers of non-judgment
settle in waves of compassion
where once were words of condemnation
Time and actions held still
for one breathless moment
that second it takes. . . going down inside
to come from the center. . . the force
where once was the warrior of fire
now waits the warrior of peace
acceptance of all that is. . . that man can do
Love conquers all without condition
one step up the pagoda
one step forward on the path
Moving silently by the humaness of struggles unmet
find the harmony within
have discord with no man
turning half aside as anger passes softly by
breath returns with the filling of the core
and non-resistance which moves the earth
has gone unnoticed as a forgotten echo
in the sound of silence
as all things change. . . peace returns

**S**ometimes you must do
that which must be done
that which is most difficult
receiving no reward
no recognition
DO IT

**Y**OU WILL BE BETTER
ONLY BY HANDLING WISELY
WHO YOU ARE NOW

Take charge of your life
set your goals
think through all problems
act upon decision
Indecision splits your power
setting you adrift. . . to tumble
down to depression. . . up to rage
progress is slowed. . . success ungained
Take command of your life
meet each challenge one at a time
be prepared to lose and you will win
do not want and you will receive
simply accept that peace and happiness
are already yours
know that all is perfect. . . in right order
time is yours. . . as is the plan you choose
Take charge now
with a clear firm voice
speak your words of truth
you are responsible only for your own life
take charge. . . take command. . . move on
all is yours
reach out

Sterling... shining
richness of all possible
future newness

I CAN

Change all ways rewarding
build all strengths restoring
keep that which is working
share that which I'm knowing

Pointed sabre straight

I CAN

Follow my freedom
love my people
open my God myself
soar to the end this time

I CAN

Grow to Infinite Oneness
evolve... returning
sterling... shining

Change will come in its own time
if what you want now does not come easily
move on to new ideas and actions
you can not force the timing of the plan of life
change yourself in this moment
so you are not slowed in progress and growth
If you are to have that desired dream
which seems at present to come so hard
step out and alter life around you
coming back another time
to what you may have missed
if it is to be yours. . . it will then be
Should it still not be in the plan this soon
continue to ask in Universal Light
keeping, always, hope and belief of the heart
for request of intent wins all
and believers are never denied

**W**hen you seek the truth
you must go to the source
At present you are seeking the truth about me
therefore I am the source
Those people who have spoken to you about me
have told you the truth about themselves
not the truth about me . . .
What is it you wish to know?

DO NOT FEAR WHAT IS AHEAD
FOR YOU WILL KNOW THE FUTURE ONLY
WHEN IT BECOMES THE NOW

You cannot rush
the natural sequence
of the events of your life
simply because one
is out of alignment

Release and consent visualize your future
say what you want and see that it is yours
Do not fear change in your life
realize the giving up of all that is old
brings newness into your reach
Release and consent
to wisdom and power greater than yours
believe that what you mean to become
is your divine right to be
That which you mean to have
already is your possession
Release
Consent

**D**o not fear rejection
what you are feeling
others feel also
some cannot make the move
to be the first to touch
Open your arms
and pull them in
though they may not respond
to your degree
you have made a difference
in their day
a difference
in their lives

Amber days barely touching fields
planting seeds of gold and mixed hues of pink
as a soft woman's wind engulfs the land
never missing its mark
on the earth or the human heart
Machinery, sinew and will
working together, striving, sharing, listening
as powers of androgynous fusion
lock into the land and into all others
Joining
for love... for good... for freedom
Merging
for God... for honor... for growth
These days of wisdom winning
remain forevermore... never to be taken
yet shared again in silence of future moments
The prophets conquer... courage stands out
Noble stature of the women
greater than the hills which surround them
is known as greatness
by the greatness of Spirit

**A**t times
we do not speak our minds
or follow our own course of action
because we do not feel self sufficient enough
to stand alone
At times
we wrap ourselves too much
into the lives and desires of those around us

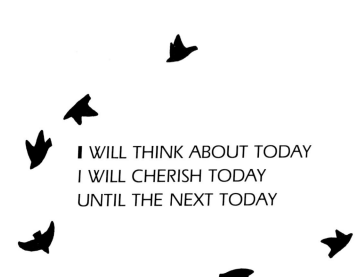

I WILL THINK ABOUT TODAY
I WILL CHERISH TODAY
UNTIL THE NEXT TODAY

Child of fire and flight you were not free
days your wanderings paced . . . existing
nights hung from the branches of the cross
trust gone . . . you were left to search
the corners of your life . . . no one was there
Your mind had taken you to beat the winds
scrape your graceful wings along the ground
you could not fly . . . I could not see you in the dust
nor did you see me . . . nor did you hear my call
"I am here . . . I am here" . . . reach up
take my hand . . . your head against my breast
I'll rock your suffering in gentleness
stroke your face and kiss the tears
of years of loveless quest . . . show yourself
before I see you pass light as light
beyond my care too far to be called back

You are in command
having a power
hidden from all but yourself
use that power wisely
begin within your mind
bring energy to rise up the center
through the top of your head
showering softly around you
making certain it touches all others
with love, kindness, patience and wisdom
Be aware of the needs of everyone
if you cannot meet those needs
do not disturb them
for time will change
coming back to you
You will require the same
from another . . .
that he use wisely
his hidden power within
to treat you
as you have treated him

# THE JOURNEY

# THE JOURNEY

Throughout these days and years of quest we encounter many teachers, prophets and masters. We have a time of service, during which we serve and attend these teachers, speakers and writers who teach us the Universal Laws to higher consciousness. We have a time when we honor the leaders who teach us to leave the rigidity of the oak and to bend, as the willow, with the flow of life. This is the time of the gathering in of wisdom of the ages. . . the wisdom of the Perennial Philosophy. From this gathering in follows the letting go of all negative energy of thoughts, feelings, words and actions. It is here that we begin our rise toward enlightenment. It is here that we abandon and leave, forever, the games and deceptions of society. This is the time of releasing, paring down, reshaping old habit patterns to enable us to allow the entrance of simplicity into our lives. . . to assimilate and use the lesson that "Everything comes and goes and nothing should matter very much."

It is a truth that "The will of God shall not take us where the grace of God cannot keep us". That time and action between will and grace is the journey. The journey begins at our beginning and ends at our ending. The track of the journey is "The Path" or "The Way."

For some of us the journey is made difficult due to the inability to surrender to the Higher Power. For some the journey is even abandoned due to an unwillingness to change and the fear of loss of all kinds. Specifically, we fear loss of people and all that which is familiar. These seekers either have forgotten, or have never known, that once one door is closed behind them, another (more fulfilling) door opens before them. And with continued moving forward and up on the path, there is a gentle guiding and lifting up to a more peaceful place of being. . . of knowing. This place is where we reside in grace, where the laws are lived not merely spoken. This place is where life is created one step at a time for the realization of a joyous, full, and peace filled life of acceptance of all the good and only the good which is desired for us, and offered to us, by our Higher Power. God is our source. No one and nothing rules our actions. Only we rule our own lives and all for which we ask comes from God, the Higher Power, the Universe. We have only to ask, and we *must* ask. After the asking, we must then trust, believing that our request is already answered and that, for which we have asked, is now ours. We then accept all good which comes to us.

During our journey we will begin to leave our teachers, books and masters. We will increase our trust in God and in ourselves until, finally, we begin to trust completely our own wisdom and our own ability to receive information directly from the Source. It is then that we come closer to the period of grace. . . blessing always the written and spoken words which nurtured the blossoming of our being. . . the slow beginnings of hearing the soft voice within our own core. This voice needs no validation from ones incarnate on this plane. We simply "know." And what we "know" is the simplicity of life.

We had begun with the many words, the concepts from outer sources, written and spoken. We finally reach, near the end of the journey, the fine tuning of our own simplicity. The letting go process, once begun, brings us to the fusion of the Oneness of all that is. We rest there in the state of grace . . . enlightenment . . . the filling and surrounding of our being with the golden light's glow.

DO NOT TURN
TAKE YOUR MEMORIES
MOVING ONLY FORWARD

**T**hrough choice and will
the journey traveled . . .
grace brings restful love
SO IT IS
IT IS SO

Something of value
that which lies closest to your heart
you give to me with commitment
no less of value I return your offering
with that which has marked my years
through daily reverence the constant respect
nurtured friendship. . . hours of experience
the ties of crystal bonding lifelines
You give me your trust
I give you my time
as all else apart. . . nothing else matters
these without question are ultimate sharing
from our depth of Oneness and giving
treasures lying deep in our silence
come forth now one to the other quietly solid
treasures which each of us knows
as something so precious
our one thing protected
our something of value

Today I journey toward wholeness
having touched the hands and hearts
of those around me
we are the same
within our differences
yet I must touch my own soul first
fill myself with strengths
necessary for the joining
of all the bodies of my body
I will make myself whole
then move into the world
to offer service for unity
of the people. . . one to the other
passing wisdom and love
through caring
sharing in the creation of Oneness
gathering each soul I meet
into my sphere of joy
We will grow together
as we advance into the future
side by side
on separate paths

. . . and if I should cry with you
would you hold me close
being silent as despair flows through
to change heaviness to light freedom
or would you only pat me
telling all the reasons not to weep
that it will be all right. . . there there. . .
I would like to try with you
as tears come so hard into my life
they simply stay a pain so tight
searing a coal-hot wound through my heart
my need is to know
if I should cry with you
would you hold me close
in silence. . .

Though your heart be still so tender
in its healing
from the pain of judgments passed
it has repaired at least this much
from the time of its bleeding throb
your mind has always known judgment
It is a game some must play
to raise themselves in esteem
in their own and others eyes
These are the ones who need your loving heart
you cannot escape harsh judgment
from the few . . . it is their way
So bless them as they pass through it
then turn to the many who love you
as you were, as you are, as you grow
and bless these as you go together
hand to hand supporting each other
in the clear pink light of love
Lift them as the changes come
heart with heart moving upward
to the bright white light
of knowing

It would be so much harder
without you

It would be so much easier
without you

SO LIFE IS

We are given the blessing
of this passage through time and space
never too far apart
that our hands do not touch
Wherever we may wander
we go with love

In your eyes
there is something more and beyond
All the things you know and feel
questions of times you have not yet had
answers to experience only you have known
flickers of pain which are quickly caught
to put back inside your control
Wonder comes through as you look at me
asking for knowledge of who I am
then an invitation to come with you
into your eyes
your mysterious magic psyche
It could be that we might find
we cannot be together there
our differences are so great
yet we need to see
if in that hidden quiet space
it could be that we can share and grow
giving each other a new kind of love
of loving
there in an aura of gentle light
joined in each other's arms behind your eyes
we may discover another place to be

Though we may not be together
times will come when we pass in space
as we perform our work
of same or different nature
and we will know that we have traveled
near to each other
though we try to detour pain
times will come when we feel its sabre cut
as memories flash in mind
Our hearts then with certainty
will send small and ancient spheres of love
to touch each other's light

Your faults and mine
the mistakes we all make
are hard to own
still harder to admit
If I want to say "I was wrong"
I am afraid you will take advantage
not let me face the fault and move on
There is a fear that you will use my words
now and then... or more often...
for your own gain or excuse
But if we both can make admission
to the humaness and constant naturalness
of individual weakness
if we are gentle in our response to acceptance
of the other's stated misdeed
I to you... you to me
we will pass easily into the comfort
of knowing we both are equal
Each of us will grow
not being held back by petty insistence
from the other to redeem ourselves
for every small slight or negligence
It takes the two of us to make it work
come try with me
once more

**W**e are never really free . . . even in death
we continue to evolve
living in the Universe
The kind of freedom we say we want
does not exist . . . and if it did
we would not know how
to be ourselves within it
We are only truly free
within the disciplines of self
and the change and growth
brought about by these realizations

Love rush
pouring out and pouring in
at times of need
reaching out to feel the touch
of hand and heart
as calm washes the soul
in firm embrace long held
No quicker healing than the arms
of a friend

Love rush
interweaving exchange of words
temporarily forgotten concepts
renewed as softly spoken truths
pass the same lips that kiss the tears
raising Divine Spirit
to its accustomed place of knowing
no more glorious healing than love
friend to friend

So much could have been ours
had you known the worth of love
its total commitment. . . the giving
even more the receiving. . . feeling
If you'd learned how to laugh
finding joy in each new morning
So much should have been ours
had you known the worth of love
offered to you openly. . . honestly
from the depth of the soul of love
Your life would have lightened
spirit rising. . . revolving in the sun
So much we would have shared
had you known the worth of love

Often golden lures belonging
in concept, article, or experience
tempt us to possess magnitudes
of material or spiritual greatness
There is desire to gather in and hold on to
all that which touches our lives
tangible or intangible. We are too fond
of deeds we are performing and people we love
Yet, none of these parts of our journey
are to be held, nor owned
for the more we let go the greater the growth
and, we keep only that which we give away
while those things to which we cling
fade as transparencies lost in the outer forever
Non-attachment becomes the strongest bond
of commitment to the freedom of enlightenment
which also must be released
as the lesson cuts through
as each phase of our time comes and goes
The more we know the less we retain
as discipline comes with the giving away
of all that passes through our awareness
We walk the path of the Middle Way
seeking. . . learning in the quest for silence
in which throbs the echo of Divine Presence
sound of forever. . . here from the gathering in
must follow the letting go
Lesson upon lesson
in the inverted vortex of evolvement
travelers to the final space of nothingness
where all things are found
from which nothing is taken
Resting there empty of all golden gifts
in the wordless void of all that is
having filled the crucible to the top of empty
the Original Way. . . The Path. . . the Suchness
we return full circle
where everything has changed
where nothing has changed
where always we are and have been
non-attached masters solidly unseen unheard
yet known for knowing by others who know

# THE GRACE

There is the silence of grace. The time of knowing who we are and knowing that we *do* "know". This is the period of living the laws through direct contact with the higher power. Everything that comes to our "inner knowing" comes from the Source. We have no need to explain ourselves to anyone. There is no need to tell others what we know. Instead, we show our inner peace through our actions in the world around us. We live the laws, free from judgment, free from fear and resentment. We are who we are, having the ability to live in society with quiet stature. Thus, we are not driven to prove our worth or our serenity. This is our time to simply show gracious kindness to all.

Living the truths of the Perennial Philosophy brings to us the gift of silence. We are able to stand with all people, together or separately, in graceful calm, enjoying all that is our divine right for joyous and prosperous living.

The society and universe in which we live have their many frustrations and challenges. We are responsible only for ourselves and our actions in this life. However, reaching the state of grace does not give us license to escape from interaction with others. For it is in this state of grace that we will find our greatest power of sharing, with all people, through example. We serve no man by assuming that we are on such a high level of spirituality that we are untouchable.

This is perhaps the level on which we most fully demonstrate our humaness. With greatest simplicity we move through humanity. With utmost quiet we move about in the world. We are free in this state of grace. Love and truth are the banners which go before us. Anger, fear and defensiveness fall away. There is no compelling urge to boast or "flash" what knowing has been attained. We are truth and light.

There is sometimes bliss. . . sometimes a flood of love through the heart center which takes breath away and sends positive love energy flowing, far reaching, to all forms of life. And, for this giving we receive. For this channeling of the Godforce we are renewed. Grace opens all senses on all levels for the clear pure Universal Truth. We are blessed as we give our blessings.

Evolvement continues. The more we know the more we know there is to know. The less we say. . . the more we know there is less that need be said. Each one of us will find his or her own truth and guidance. Each one of us will evolve in his or her own divine time. Each one will come to rest from the power of the will, through the strength of the journey, to the gentle silence of grace.

For all of us on the path, we offer to each other and share a soft and powerful courage. Be at peace, beloved souls.

Healing Light
touch gently on sand and sea
Gather from the elements your strength
Soar with the wind
flashing colors as you revolve
in the fire of reflecting sun

      This is the moment of your power
      This is your humility

**M**iracles brought forth from each other
responses to knowing
a single word spoken. . . a gesture
merely an hour spent intensely shared
one person's time dedicated solely to another
Love
the healer beyond all words, transcending action
what the Spirit knows above what mind can think
Truth in giving and receiving of the Light
color ringing vibration. . . sound changing structure
Gently the touching of hands calls forth
one small glowing globe of perfect health
deep within. . . and untouched by the world
True wellness from the true self
the Godforce unleashed in wonder and certainty
Always it was there hidden in protection
from the angers of the world. . . safe from the rest
until the Soul was ready to accept ideas
of change spoken through encouraging love
To be free
Finally casting off all limitation of pain
disease retreats as do injury and weakness
and one small glowing globe grows

replacing all negative energy
of inner and outer self
God is the healer
as that energy is the Source of all good
Once the knowing has risen to be recognized
nothing learned can be unlearned
there is no turning back . . . and wellness physically
mentally, emotionally, spiritually, socially
has set new directions for one more soul
on the path of miracles
It is the Source you know
the Force each being seeks
as one human channel passes to another
that same Golden Light
which was received the hour before
Miracles we bring to each other
as fish and bread there are plenty for all
Love spirals through humanity unseen
yet felt by all . . . one hour in each lifetime
the time of the rising of brothers and sisters
nothing wanting . . . no one crying
Find your hour and turn to another
Love
the Force
Healing Miracle

**T**HERE IS THAT WHICH IS YOURS ALONE
IT IS THE QUALITY OF LIGHT OF YOUR HEART
BE TRUE TO IT
SHINE IT FOR ALL TO SEE
AS IT RETURNS BRINGING RADIANCE
FROM ALL HEARTS SURROUNDING YOU
YOU KNOW . . . THERE IS LOVE

**G**reat Spiritual Power of the Universe
turn your sun on my life
that I may reflect it back
to You

Moonlight rays in brilliance
white flashing lightening cracks
as the storms of our lives pass through
one by one
as the struggle of the stone of Sisyphus
positive action now prevails
though we may falter some . . . time to time
never do we fall back . . . only pause for breath
filling each cell with energies needed
fortifying our beings
with the thunderhead's power
coming into alpha under deep sky blue
Sunlight rays in brilliance
warming each fiber . . . each atom
energizing, purifying the inner and outer
as warmth seeks its level
from the heart to the sun
and the fire of power and strength
rises from the base touching each vortex
bringing in turn balance to calm
Those which appear as storms of violence
are merely fuel for the journey toward peace
Moonlight . . . Sunlight
Spiritual rays in brilliance
We are the Light
in joy and love we stand shining
in brilliance

Peace of here and hereafter
knowing there is abundance of time
Looking back . . . the footprints
lead to where we stand this moment
looking forward . . . the footprints
lead to where we are destined to be
Time between is ours . . . is present . . .
the plan is set, we need only follow
Time is full of freedom to be
to accept, surrender, let go
Time is the tool of now . . . tool of the future
God stretches time non-existent
into space non-existent
and the use of both is but the knowing
we can not make a mistake
only . . . will we succeed in all that is ours to do
Pressure to produce is lifted from us
we are free to move in comfort
in peaceful harmony with our days
Time is friend and ally . . . comforting
removing all necessity, all rules
Standing out, clearly, time open-ended
unbounded . . . is breadth, depth
the vehicle which carries us to
each ending of each segment
of this and every other life
Time is our empty full void
the unreality which we use by seconds
never remembering it is not there
yet soaring to our glory
on its transparent wings

It is between two flowing
soft light colors carrying
love from your heart
warmth from your hands
In this moment of silence
you open yourself to give
receiving from the field around you
Your intent the passage
of courage and self discovery
releasing energy, guiding awareness
merging with time and each other
as the Universe surrounds your space
For this intense sharing time stops
you see. . . you know. . .
you are God
as the Spirit comes through you
Healer you are Divine Love
        You are Infinite

Trust me beyond what you can reason
fear not that you will be betrayed
Never is there a certainty for security
and nothing worthwhile is ever gained
without the holy risk taken
Trust me beyond that which you have seen
for only time and experiences shared
can bring the necessary quality of feeling
knowing that you are safe in my presence
that the innermost you is protected
Trust me beyond your sacred self
You have revealed nothing that will expose you
and I am here for reassurance that all is well
You are not alone in your concerns
over past expressions
Trust that what I say is so for many
We all have committed acts which we fear
have held us from progress on our path
yet all acts, thoughts, feelings and words
are part of the plan
foundations for future excellence
Trust me
I bring this confidence from a Higher Power
The stone you carry constantly
is now to be released
placed as the corner stone
of the temple for yourself
within whose walls
will vibrate, reverberate, trust
Assimilation and union has taken place and
"Trust me" are merely two words you used to hear
before fear left you at the bridge of truth
so that you might cross over for eternity
into the soothing, comfortable, productive world
of security and peace, the unconditional love
resting forever
in the circulating unending constant
Trust me in the known and in the unknown
Trust me
Trust

I'll walk with you to the cypress tree
past the lemon grove and olive
along dirt paths of filtered dust
through which shimmer ancient faces
following footsteps of the wise and inspired
touching our sandals to the many prints
of the poor and the gentle . . . the infirmed
I'll walk with you to the cypress tree
which we planted as children and nurtured
as we kept very busy
away from disturbing the white robed elders
as they spoke of Masters . . . and of One
who shone most brightly in love
in light and truth . . . in controversy
I'll walk with you to the cypress tree
past the date palms to the stone well
There we will fill each jar serenely
mixing water and prana of equal parts
for cleansing of body and soul
quenching our thirst for life and wisdom
for healing exchange in silence
I'll walk with you to the cypress tree
but there, this time, I shall leave you
There before parting we will seek the depth
of each other's eyes . . . to the core of our knowing
Our paths will diverge in swirls of dust
without looking back . . . hands raised
in pause and farewell
We'll meet again some other lifetime
past the rows of trees
by the cypress

You are the Christ
as am I
You know your own Christedness
as I know mine
yet I do not know you in flesh
I know you as brother and sister
We have known each other's pain
in growing, in sharing, in teaching
and in the risk of difference
of standing out in the world
to speak "I AM"
of reaching out in the world
to heal another
of stepping out in the world
to lead the seekers
I know your Christedness
as I know mine
We have been the Christ together
for thousands of years
I have seen you weep my tears

as I have shed your blood
We have shared the Light between us
for our own healing
Now with our hands held by each other
we rise again in Spirit
joy in soul, love pulsing our hearts
We rise once more accepting our way
striding out on our path
our path of old. . . with always new direction
strong. . . well. . . silent. . . joyous. . . loving
with compassion and understanding for all
I hail the Christ within you
and offer my honor to your being
I accept the power of your salutation returned
I shall see you in the ethers
and hold you in my knowing
we are One in all eternity
Our Christ. . . our God. . . our Universe
Our Oneness. . . lighting the way
Our silence forever heard

To right the wrong
gliding from end to end of feeling
renewing, once more, understanding for another
To right the wrong and love on
coming back in peace and Oneness
in times together following conflict
beloved with beloved rising above adversity
beyond accusation. . . to the heart
moving to soul level depth
still flowing full core length
Knowing. . . anger which has been spoken
is surface level and shallow
Knowing. . . undesired deeds performed
have faded already in time
To right the wrong
with a touch of softness
carrying the Godforce of love
healing the pain of separation
with this lifetime love's intensity
'Tis a special flight of heart
exchanging with each other
tenderness from patience to forgiveness
To right the wrong and love on

**W**aves whispered on the shore yesterday
you heard them. . . I hear them now
as sounds hang in the atmosphere
you'll hear them when you are gone
for you must go. And we know
as the mists above the water hang tonight
tomorrow you will be a part of every drop
As souls live on, yours will mingle with the mist
and I shall see you each night, light on the grass
touching petals in the morning. You'll be there
I would hold you to life though it is not mine
to change the course of your pattern. To go
or stay was once your choice
but now the whisper fades
as you go with it to another shore
I can only stand as tides recede
life following along
Time has come and gone as planned

Do you hear the things I say
Find me as your shelter
when fear in your mind comes too hard
Seek my warmth when you feel small and cry
Mingle your thought and heart with mine
if confusion has you running
Share my strength when you feel
crushed by the world
Hear me. . . I am here for you
Touch me. . . I will not disappear
under the onslaught of your being human
See me
Accept from me
Know me

Celebration
ringing strains of all sustained sound
from cold tempered metals across the Himalayas
Tibetan bells . . . nothing more
Pulsations oscillating in widening ringlets
purifying the way of travelers
cleansing vibrations going before the seekers
opening the path for pilgrims of truth
The way of truth can not be denied
Law upon Law opening life
creating abundance . . . strengthening the heart
Rewards for willingness to change
are many and great requiring only acceptance
Be ready, know your worth, receive your gifts
So insistently all ringing lingers
echoes in labyrinths of the ear
causing wonder to question its reality
For your spirit rising . . . know now
it is Tibetan bells . . . nothing more
Striding forward the path is steep
steady gain affording clearer air
Taking each breath away bringing ringing anew
from four equidistant directions
waves of vibration
sound so light it pains the ear
so loudly constant it is scarcely heard
compelling tones drawing souls upward
along stairs of gold where ethers resound
to join all beauty of sound in Celestial Harmony
Somewhere amid this ancient splendor
you know the truth as it began
some lifetimes ago . . . each knowing heart is cleared
by Tibetan bells . . . nothing more
All of this belongs to you
all of this has gone before
music for enlightenment
nothing more

WE MAY RECEIVE FROM EACH OTHER
THAT WHICH WE FIND IN EACH OTHER

Because we cannot see
inside the heart of another
never will we know
the total truth which rests there
We will be shown only that
which the other chooses to reveal
at the selected time of disclosure

You are here
beamed from the Higher Force
A light most brilliant of clarity and balance
origins from Oneness... most powerful fragment
many have fallen before you anointing your feet
many have risen before you accepting your love
You have been here always
guiding the Universe... Master of masters
no matter your age or miracle
All is nothing except the Christedness of you
through which flows the Godforce of love
as the Oneness shines a multitude of rays
light to coalesce and heal all people
None is the lesser, none the greater
We are brothers and sisters of singular energy
the path is narrow, the stairway steep
All is ours in the name of God, Christ and Spirit
We ask of you
love through the flame which burns in our hearts
through love intensify the heat to purify
speak your word, raise your hand and lift us
for we know you are here
In surrender we commit to serve you
great prophet... tender healer... wise teacher
pass down through time and space
of the infinite void
all those things which we will be
Bless us in our trust in your truth
touch us with your holiness as we reflect
back to you your radiance
enfold us in the Oneness... the Suchness
as we ebb and flow in the ethers
of our only God... as we know
You are here and always have been
we hail, we behold
our Christ
in all things

People of the ages... seers and prophets
people of the ages put your hands out
touch beyond your reach
moving past limitation
past the many voices who bid you stay
who bid you move to common tempo
those voices with words of direction
droning that their way is the only way
People of the ages of the Universe
there are no absolutes
each knowing today may become new
as information changes
each knowing today will grow
to become change... or return
People of Light of Spirit
move past limitation of thought
think not that this is all there is

that this which man has created
man must tend to . . . it is not so
There is no limitation
and this which man has created
comes through man form the Higher Source
the power of that Source tends to all matters
Let go your chains. . . now
rise to the limitless boundless soaring
of open ended everchanging free thought
. . . what the Spirit knows. . .
create life with joyous imagination
know that all is now given
and nothing which is yours
can ever be taken from you
God is your Source
in eternity. . . in infinity
all is One. . . as are you

New hope and direction are yours
never lost only put by on occasion
Lives you have touched with your heart
have not gone uneffected
for it takes but one gesture
during anyone's lifetime
the right person at the crucial moment
and a flower opens unto the world
Blossoms you have offered to God
will return to the warmth of your Soul
staying nearby in your solitude
traveling with you on your path
brightening the way of your direction
rejoicing in the light of your hope

You shelter me
when all seems to fail
You cover me
when I have done my work
and I'm feeling small
You answer me
when I've called your name
Not always do I know at once
that you have heard me
Yet you cover me in healing light
Your presence enters my heart
drawing me into shelter of the Oneness
My journey into your silence
returns the waning strength
I remain yours
channel. . . instrument. . . servant
I am of you, my Master
you shelter me as I have asked
as I let you light the way
You shelter me
You cover me
and I am blessed

Restless spirit finally stilled
by quiet constant patience of love
a presence known though unseen
So right this gift given in the touch of silence
revolving sharing returning unending
just beginning now in karmic timing
Grateful, this restless spirit
for the tenderness of a field from the past
supple undulating energies familiar
never again to separate or lose
that which was again is
Calm, peace, serenity channeled
for future great powers. The discipline
flowing forth bonded in kindest care
Covering. . . the sweet lotus petals
float above in cool green waters
gentling this restless spirit
far within the depths of years
guiding from intensity into peace at last

When I saw your hands
so light and slightly arched
tapered fingers through which flows life
energy from the Universe
strength from your heart and love
the life flow channeling so quietly
showed only on your face
and in the light glow around you
I loved you then
a feeling deep unending
That silent unseen flow of life
came through you into me
in days past
giving courage, hope and future
In that minute . . . and just as silently
tears fell behind my eyes
into the blue of my etheric body
Only these things mattered at that moment
my tears . . . your hands . . . and love

**B**rotherhood and womanhood
multitudes and millions
strands of angels threading heavenward
touching wingtips, hands outstretched
a golden glow to light the way
This, our celestial display of Oneness
with the blending of the light
shines one continuing sustaining radiance
humanity is cast in gold
on this plane of earth
vibration transmits from heart to heart
multitudes become a single being
millions now are only one
There is no separation of God and Human
grace is given to us all
every step imprints in Eternity
all words spoken carry through the Universe
as a sound which has no sound
Joining our hands with brothers and sisters
reaching to touch the angel wings
our reward will come as we know it
in the silence of our stillness
So softly we rise in merging colors
chanting mingling with bells ringing
mysteries dissolved as distances diminish
angel threads encompass our world
stretching beyond the sky and the void
Grace has reached our souls at last
every answer has been given
to the questions never asked
we may join the strands of angels
fusing our tranquility with theirs
Hearts at peace and souls in grace
there is nothing left but light
resting now multitudes and millions
forever One with Brotherhood
with Womanhood

The final knowing
of our awareness
will be . . .
that we have walked
only with Angels
and come to completion
with only One Master

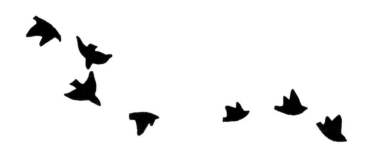

# ABOUT THE AUTHOR

Warmth, gentleness, courage, caring and giving are words which immediately come to mind when one hears the name Diane Westlake. She is truly a unique individual who shares her insights and love for others through the written and spoken word. Diane teaches and speaks to groups on the Universal Laws, the personal spiritual growth of individuals, wellness and the Holistic life style.

Born and raised on the Southern California coast, Diane lived an active life of vitality and health. She graduated from UCLA, taught in the California secondary schools for 22 years, raised her son Michael, and now enjoys the pleasures of her three grandchildren.

*The Will and the Grace* is Diane's third book. At the time of her first book, in 1977, she was living a disabled life as a result of crippling arthritis. Through counseling, energy balancing, love, support and the positive thoughts of many true, dependable friends, she reversed the disease and now lives as the strong, athletic woman she had been.

Having chosen a lifetime of service to others, Diane prayed to be allowed to continue to serve even though she had been told she would never recover from arthritis. Her prayers were answered, she was given her own wellness and now follows her personal "spiritual calling" through her written and spoken words. She is published internationally in both poetry and in articles which she wrote, for more than a year, for an Australian journal of health and healing.

Diane's full life experiences and deep spirituality lend themselves to the truth and compassion of her words. She teaches, guides and brings peace, calm and simplicity through the skillful use of her words. She brings a gift to the world as she believes she herself has been given many loving and true gifts from all others who have touched her life.